ACTS AS BOLD AS LOVE

First published in 2025 by TheNeverPress

A CIP record of this book is available from the British Library.

ISBN 9781999653057

Cover design by Graham Thomas & Annie Couldrey

@TheNeverPress

www.theneverpress.com

YOU ARE ALWAYS THERE.
INSIDE.
TENDING TO MY LANTERN.

ACTS

AS

BOLD

AS

LOVE

ACTS AS BOLD AS LOVE

The Overview Effect

I am in orbit around you for the first time
And nothing will be the same again
You sent me into your upper atmosphere
With little warning after the fervent sex
And giggles that kissed me on the launchpad
I took off and left behind what I didn't know
You were the ground all along
And now I am floating up in space
But not alone
How many have been here? How many before me?
What would I call those that are now my ancestors
Those who were launched into orbit like me
We are so connected. Me to them. We to you.
All of us a network of fluid and fucking
It's profound and scary up here
I want to come home now
Bring down my capsule
Give me fifteen minutes
Then kiss me on that launchpad again

All in Stride

Countless days are clouds
They scud across my view
I blow kisses to each day
The breeze indifferent
Because I am indifferent
Everything marches
Everything is a soldier
Everything is a war
And I am indifferent
Because as it all scuds across my view
And days are counted up as years
Years rounded up to the nearest life
It all marches on by me
And I'll just sit

Alone

You've teleported,
You've evaporated away,
Disintegrated and gone.

And all that's left,
Those stale flip flops,
Footprints of you

I can't touch them,
Sacrosanct artefact,
Achingly in view.

Abandoned like me
As you beamed aboard
Signatory and left,

I am so sadly dead,
So monstrously adrift,
Please hurry back from CoOp

Flower-Strewn

Not a funeral and not for the dads
Not tearfully dusting lonesome lily pads

Or a garden or some wreath laid bare
Flowers strewn neither here or there

Root and stem, supple tender blooms
Each one vined to enclose vaulted rooms

Things to say and things to do
Grown from soil to make it through

But my chance has gone, now entombed
Hopes now fetid petals old
... eschewed

The Navigator

You're changing shape
I have charted it all
From this little island here
To the next little island there

Your tectonic plates are shifting
Only you can see it
And only I can love it
Storm if you will, I'll just sail

Your volcanic core isn't stable
So I charter your curves
For my private maps
Happy to navigate the surface

Underneath I've not the mettle
Nous or instruments
To chart and to know
That maelstrom, your soul

Zubaida

I was always asking after you,
Sending a wink
Hoping through boozy days
That my ship would come in
But you were so landlocked,
Iraqi desert cooly aloof
I was no Lawrence or anything new
But Holy living hell,
We found each other
In one way or another
You cried at the film
And privately informed
The loss and the pain.
How come you're so light?
So peppy and zippy
With depth like tar
I wonder about you; all your ways
Infinite interests,
And your Air Max library
I think most times
You and I will die
I don't want it... but confess
You and me in heaven?
Fuck, what a sesh

Brighton

Baby, love, light
I am so calm in nature
So calm around you,
I am all of this
And more of that
A geo-stationary orbit around you
Baby, love, light
I am so happy, giggly
So teeny around you
You have a thing
I have a thing
We have a thing
And the trains are running,
Imagine that!
A time to feel alive,
And what a world,
Melded in a Brighton bed

He Is Away Now

So trill and bright, a poet is lost!
Gone and gone, we soak in tears
And wring our hands until they dry
We mangle the eulogy, and oh!
We're prone now to despondency
Everything hurts, time is a queue for misery

And yet the trill that I hear while
I swoon upon the moonlit sill
The pain of my sad-song whale
Inside kissed abed
As I then look to my hand
For there so bright, the poet lands
So trill! And bright!
Behold! A nightingale!

Left to My Devices

You got to give me love
In any and all forms
Don't touch me
You got to give me love
I need all of you
Maybe your glance
Or a sneeze
Just my way, I need your love
Just don't touch me
You got to give me love
I cry and squeal for it all
Don't leave me alone
I am so tired and far away
Nobody seems to see
The forgotten me
The place to have been seen
Is now no longer evergreen
But dust
So bleak
This is what happens when you don't
Give me love
You gotta give me love

November

One hour in November
Was cold and loveless around
Your skin rebelling against you
Pulled your collar to the side
And I saw your ashtray neck
Our four eyes are glass

One minute in November
I was cold and bored all over
You held yourself tightly
Trying to keep together
Nothing is yours you said
I poured ambivalent coffee

One second in November
When it meant nothing at all
Your vacuum soul sighed
At least I thought I heard so
You stared down at the table
As I prepared my goodbye

Your voice hasn't been heard
Since I left you at table
When the cheque arrived
I stood and left you alone
When I should have stayed
One eternity in November

Opal

There is a life within
That I cannot touch,
Like the one outside,
Stardust and milky,

I never was a hot one
For the romance or stuff,
Just the brood in the back,
In the corner afraid

But enough of all that
Sadness cannot fit
Not if I am to win you
And make sexy mistakes

From the corner I come
And ask you straight up
Leave the husband behind,
We can be sad in bed.

The Ballad of Old Tick Tock

He kicks his heels in the doorway,
Teaches himself tricks with a yoyo,
Practices cartwheels and cat's cradle

He plays patience and solitaire
He throws a baseball against the wall
Catching it in a glove and over again

Like that movie star he knows they all know

He paces up and down
He drums the table
He counts to infinity
And back to zero

He occupies your call time
As best as he can
Waiting around, bored to tears
Because he has something to do
A place to take her
Somewhere to go
Somewhere hot for Ava
But she won't hurry up
She fucking takes her sweet time
Ava just don't want to die

He has got all of infinity
But he hasn't got all day
Ava, she just wants to live
Tick
Tock
Tick
Tock

Szilvia

Some days the bed is on fire
And I leap with verve
To commit to task
Recreation of various ways
To recapture, and keep, your violet heart

Some days the bed is a gaol
And I'm shackled
I pick the locks with tears
And leave bed to complete various chores
To keep our home clean and happy
(Though my standards will never meet yours)

It is true that I am so tired
Too tired for sleep
My sadness is a well
Without an echo
But I can never turn away
Though I will not let go
Because I have loved you
Since the very time I saw you
All those years ago
And across the way

Ava Monro

There are winds four,
Hearts of elemental loves
Into her hair they reach
Where there they stretch
Relaxing into zephyr's peace

There is ground laid bare,
Its desires turned soil to eat
Into her mouth, were it swills
Falling into her belly in alkaline rush
The soil and earth into her, home

There is water at ankle
From Nature's ache becomes her tears
Around her feet they cool
Where they hug the cream towers
Of her legs so brightly silk

There is girl, threshold – woman
From centuries walk to her arrive
At the gates I stand aghast
I did not ask an author for your birth
Bless'd of gifts, Ava, for here you are

The Quietist

I saw no angst in the ocean,
The black depth
I saw no trouble in the sky
The azure ether
I saw almost nothing in the magma
Primordial bore
I saw nothing of value in all
As its ocean, sky and magma
Nothing more
I am carbon
What more should need be known?
I spoke that question and smiled.
And so it was answered
And so it goes
And so the quietest went.

Share This Together

Moved around the city in dark tubes
They sigh without relent
Scampering in tunnels
Hope for sun apparently spent
Look at the faces, feel *The Nothing*
It sways with the carriage
Hang from rails or clutch to seats
Long dark death beneath the city
Share the inhale, the endless sigh
Together forgotten
Under the ground, not even maggots to eat us
We share this together
Then we step out of the dark tunnel
Into razor wind under hangover skies
And the sheet rain that beats us so hard
We plead again for the big yawn
Under the City without a dawn

The Birthday Party

Nick breaks
And Frazer lines
Then Patrick pots
And old Tim pours

Captains all,
Commanders and chiefs
Together in Autumn
To be around me

Another solar orbit
Celebrated with love
Class with a capital A
Without them... well, where?

Scaff

I am a building under construction
Plans after plans
An architect designed me
But then they died and
Some other took the plans and
Made them own
I have some foundations
They've been laid over and again
Some beams and joists
Methods and tools of names I don't know
Generations of skills have been used
To make something of me
I don't know if I will ever be finished
When the ribbon will be cut and
The scaff will come down
You're so perfect it seems to all
It's always my fault as I am only to you
Always just a building under construction

One Thousand Voices

That silence that is never what it seems
That grand old elephant in the room
Inside me one thousand voices
Every one giddy to let loose a scream

A power vacuum in the heart of my throat
A sinkhole for courage, a landfill for sighs
But with one thousand gathering voices
Boy scouts with flint sparking up some hope

One thousand voices and the mightiest inhale
The scouts become guerillas armed to the lungs
So that they can bellow out, so that they can scream
We howl to break free of this old lifer's gaol!

Magma forms our glorious design
We bust out! We lurch! We eat it all up
No grey silences in the pit of my organs
Just a clear cacophony of discordant stillness
One thousand cherubs singing an aria
I'm fucking doing alright, me

Sleep

Don't ever be far from me
Show me my dreams and worlds
Those places I long to be
The strange and the desired
Without the Northern Line
Lands and skies, opal and bronze
Take me there, to that home
Away from here, from commuter sleep
Oh! The worlds and realms you give
And how I turn to them and weep

Hold On

The lights are out and so we cross the divide
Endless sink-hole engines, inside ourselves
Across the void we close eyes and leap
With no hope ahead, nor rope to anchor
No thread or vine now tied to our home
To remind us just why we set out to go
A lighthouse we desire, a tear to remind
Just were we are heading as we cross the divide

On the Back Streets of Kanazawa

Rusted air con units and propane tanks
Stacked against weeping shacks
So through the winding little streets
From the museum of gold leaf trinkets
She retreats
Back through the rain, again
With every footstep that she takes
With her every heart beat she breaks
She walks through the rain, again
Back to the hotel by the station
Where no lover waits in her bed
But instead the conference that she attends
Through the rain she walks along
The grey wetness down her back
Towards the grey suits and grey faces in the room
To the OHP and it's dull light
To the stats and graphs and no lover in her bed
She walks
She had a lunch break of an hour
Sometime at least to walk around
The back streets of Kanazawa
But the museum was closed,
The way blocked by rain and grey
So back she walks to the hotel
By the station where no lover waits in her bed
Ava doesn't look to her left, into the dusty windows
Along the endless streets.

If she did, she'd see me there
Staring back to her.
But she doesn't, she walks on
Back to the hotel
To the grey
To the conference and the empty bed.

Weird Tides

We are weird tides
No one pushing.
No one pulling.
Just drawn.
We may drift apart for one hot second
But we never leave our water.

The Irritant

Paint me into your corners
Trap me with a blank page
Leave me with the oven on
And kick me over the fence
Calculate the annoyances
That irritant your skin
Then name me after them
So that I can be around

The Bookie

He found it very hard to love you
His pencil short and blunt
Like the words he wrote on the slip
That he labelled as a dead cert

The doubts, the odds, the nags
All these things around and around
Added up to something not so tasty
Something a drunk wouldn't bet on

It was you, from the gate, to the grave
It was never him, he said it was you
Nothing but a fucker that wasn't even good for glue

He didn't wear make-up for you
He didn't even do his nails
Because he said some things you shouldn't hear
Some things he said when you were somewhere else
Somewhere far and not so near

He's torn paper now, balled and floored
Among the lads broke and corralled
Into waste paper bins in corners
Because he bet it all and you never came in

Alejandra

The world becomes galaxies
The possibility of forever
Do you know what it means?
To be adrift in you
The Milky Way of love
It's a Voyager
A Beagle
A way beyond the light fantastic
Worlds and shakes to take you far
Around the perimeter
And to circle back to arms
In arms in arms
And legs in knots
The world becomes galaxies
And forever is QED

The Traveller

Where must we go
To be seen in our land?

What must we overturn
For hope to take root?

What climb must we endure
To secure a clear view?

What depth must we plumb
To be the photon in the void?

What air must we inhale
To then know ourselves as ourselves?

The Northern Line

I love you like crazy
It makes me so mad
In fact, people on transport
Have stopped and stared
Previously ignored (I liked it that way)
Now they all stand and stare
As I float on my cloud
I let them all on
And get the next one along
When aboard I just grin
Wide-eyed and happy
Black nails on our date
I recall it all and why
Oh, why can't they stop staring?
And excuse me a touch
It's not my fault from Morden to Edgware
I love you so much

I am ruining their commute

Sleeping Pile of Dust

I think you are sleeping, though I cannot be sure,
Your body heaves and sighs,
A ghost I guess,
Around three hours past since you said you'd sleep
Around three hours,
More or less.

If you are alive in your slumber, I just cannot tell.
Not now, not even then,
You were laughing
When your eyes shone I was sure you were awake
But alive? I just couldn't tell.

Under the light of a dead moon I turn. Revolt.
A passion opens a wide
I am a simple violent
Now that you're asleep I know for sure
Before you're dust, we shall meet Anew

While Asleep

In a winter's dream I created the sun
Below it a park where children played
And lovers lay upon the grass
And drank their wine.

I built a world and stood aghast
As everyone there went about their lives
And they spoke and laughed
But none to me.

I created warmth in that winter dream
And in a moment of inspiration divine
I cleared away the clouds
And over-saturated the sky.

It was almost perfect that place
That verdant park where children played
And for a second it was
The second after that, they came.

First the planes began to fall from my sky
Exploding on the horizon, passed the trees
And the lovers stood and spilt their wine
Children turned from their play
And the frisbees flew unattended.

The planes fell and the ships arrived
Copper whales in the azure sky
Bellies rotund, groan and ache
Distressed armada fell out of the clouds.

Then the ground shook and earth ruptured
And in my park, in my dream
The Machine Men awoke and climbed out of bed.

Sad giants, brushing off the aeons of sleep
They stretched wide and yawned, great horns
And the sun was taken from my sky

The Machine Men buckled and leaped up to their ships
Finally awake and returning to work
They left the world, they left my park.

The place I created in my winter's dream
In that sleep when I created the sun
My ancestors awoke!
And then they were gone.

ACTS

AS

BOLD

AS

LOVE

Acknowledgements

With grateful and loving thanks to my family for
their encouragement and support. To my friends, in
particular Donatella Marena, Craig Coole, Luke Searle,
Aarti Pattni, Annie Couldrey & Chris Rolfe.

To that one teacher, mentor and friend who set me
right – Mr John B Peacock – and, finally, with love and
thanks to the legends of TheNeverPress: Dave Hollander,
Tim Foley & Rosie Cook.

I love all of you more than The Cure.

About the Quiet Pilot

As a wee lad, Graham Thomas wanted to be a pilot, a butler, a film-maker and an author. The only one that really stuck with him was 'author'.

So far it seems to have worked out well for him, creatively. As well as writing novels and poetry, Graham also runs a digital zine stuffed with curios, and hosts a podcast about racehorses and movies. His eventual plan is to see out his days in a hacienda filled with animals and let the surrounding land do what she desires.

Alongside writing, Graham loves making models, cooking giant roasts, boxing, swimming, the Prince Charles Cinema and The Cure.

About TheNeverPress

TheNeverPress is an independent publishing house specialising in original print, audio and digital media including a digital magazine on the arts, and a podcast about movies and racehorses. All of it curiously off-beat and made entirely in-house with love – and likewise given.

We value our independence and plan to release a few publications each year in our own way and on our own terms: paperbacks, zines, online serialisations and podcasts – anything we can dream up, we'll make happen.

We're a collective of creatives who want to build an inclusive and curious label that is authentic, meaningful, ethical and always goes full steam.

At TheNeverPress, we are brimming with creative ideas and bursting with vision and we're eager to get more people involved: writers, artists, creatives, behind-the-scenes specialists. If you share our ideals of being independent, curious, caring and authentic, and if you see things in a different way then get in touch and let's see if we can make some cool stuff together.

Find out all about us at: **www.theneverpress.com**
Subscribe to our zine: **zine.theneverpress.com**

@TheNeverPress

www.theneverpress.com

www.ingramcontent.com/pod-product-compliance
Lightning Source LLC
Chambersburg PA
CBHW021944040426
42448CB00008B/1231